Flower Arranging Secrets

Natural Designs for Everyday Living

BY JANE GODSHALK

Photography by Tom Weishaar

Additional Photography by Ann MacMullan

Although the author has made every effort to ensure that the information in this book was correct at press time, the author does not assume and hereby disclaim any liability to any party for any loss, damage, or disruption caused by errors or omissions, whether such errors or omissions result from negligence, accident, or any other cause.

FLOWER ARRANGING SECRETS
ISBN: 978-0-9914223-0-2
Designer: Baxendell's Graphic
Editor: Pete Prown

© Jane P. Godshalk 2014

Without limiting the rights under copyright reserved above, no part of this publication may be reproduced, stored in or introduced into a retrieval system, or transmitted, in any form, or by any means (electronic, mechanical, photocopying, recording, or otherwise), without the prior written permission of the author of this book.

To Betsy, Madeline, and flower lovers across the globe.

Acknowledgments

Grateful thanks to all of my teachers, students, and flower friends who have shared in the joy of working with flowers, inspiring me to grow my love of flowers into a most satisfying career. Ann MacMullan, with her eye for design and respect for the eco-friendly way to arrange flowers, spurred the idea for "natural" arranging.

Huge thanks to Tom Weishaar for his meticulous care with photographs, skill, and enthusiasm. Book editor Pete Prown helped me keep the writing on target and designer Laurie Baxendell made it all look wonderful. Eric deserves a special thank you for his patience and generosity of spirit, and Adam for making the appreciation of nature a daily ritual.

Contents

Getting Prepared — 10
Finding flowers — 12
Vases and Containers — 16
Tools and Mechanics — 20

Planning Your Designs — 22
Space & Style — 25
Color — 26
Stem Placement — 32
Proportions — 34

The Design Studio — 37
Branches — 38
Chicken wire — 52
Sand — 62
"Lean" — 70
Hand-Tied Bouquet — 78
Fruits and Vegetables — 86

More Secrets — 94
Table Display — 96
More Color — 98
Foliage — 100

Flower identification — 102

SECRET
Setting an attractive table is easy when you let the flowers be the stars.

Enjoying flowers in your home is a simple luxury we can all afford. Flowers enhance everyday living with their constantly changing parade of colors, shapes, and textures. Even better, they are readily available from supermarkets, farmers markets and florists all year long—good news for those of us who don't have endless amounts of time to spend tending to garden plants. My own personal garden is rather small and seems to have fewer flowers each year. Instead, I grow an increasing number of plants for their interesting foliage, which will complement the excellent flowers I can easily purchase from the market.

Yet now that most of us have access to these high-quality flowers, the question may arise *What should I do next?*

The goal of *Flower Arranging Secrets* is to demystify the process of designing with flowers for your home. When I was a beginning flower arranger I found it frustrating when a book left me feeling like the plant material was too difficult to find and the designs would be difficult to achieve. This book aims to make the art of flower arranging accessible to all. I want to empower busy flower lovers like you with techniques to help quickly and easily create beautiful flower arrangements for every occasion. It is created with respect for the environment and uses local, conscientiously grown flowers whenever possible. Most of the support mechanics are also reusable or recyclable.

At the world-renowned Longwood Gardens in Kennett Square, Pennsylvania, I teach a course in beginning floral design which gives students the fundamental knowledge to create their own flower arrangements for the home. The excitement of seeing students' enthusiasm as they discover the art of arranging has been my inspiration to finally put some ideas from my classes and lectures into a book.

I truly hope you enjoy reading *Flower Arranging Secrets* as much as I did writing it.

Jane

JaneGodshalk.com

SECRET
A mix of garden flowers, house plants, and flowers from the market can work together to make a beautiful arrangement.

A floral designer's first question is "Where should I get my flowers?" You can find them from street vendors, in flower shops, supermarkets, garden stands, and farmers markets, which are becoming increasingly popular. A good first move is to raid your local grocery store. Bunches of roses, alstromeria, and seasonal flowers are readily available from supermarkets, but be picky and look for firm blossoms and buds. There should be no brown or wilted foliage (you want flowers that are either *in* bloom or *about* to bloom; keep an eye out for any that have peaked and are about to wither).

Next, ask someone on the market's staff which days the flowers are delivered and plan your purchases accordingly. When you bring flowers home from the market, they will do best if unwrapped immediately, given a fresh cut (at a slant), and put into cool water quickly.

Some flowers often available from markets are:

Spring: tulips, daffodils, lilacs
Summer: zinnias, dahlias, sunflowers,
Fall: chrysanthemums, sunflowers, field flowers
Winter: greens and pine, carnations
Any season: roses, alstromeria, calla lilies, carnations

Getting Prepared

Also, get to know a local florist who can provide you with hard-to-find supplies and special blossoms that give great impact to a design and last a long time. And certainly, having your own garden brings the opportunity to grow not only flowers, but a wide variety of trees, shrubs and foliage. This is very useful when supplementing store-bought blossoms. Your climate dictates what will be available and when, and each growing season brings its challenges and delights.

A few trees, shrubs, and perennials that can provide you with good material for your designs are:

Trees
Bradford pear for branches and fall color
Holly
Magnolia
Maple for fall foliage
Pine and cedar
Stewartia for blossoms and fall foliage

Shrubs
Acuba
Boxwood
Hydrangea
Smokebush
Variegated weigela
Viburnum

Perennial Flowers & Bulbs
Bulbs, narcissus, tulips, allium
Begonia for foliage
Clematis
Hellebores for flower and foliage
Hosta
Grasses

Houseplants & Annuals
Alocacia
Aspidistra
Begonia
Croton
Coleus
Echeveria
Variegated geraniums
Other interesting annuals

SECRET

Choose seasonal colors to bring the outdoors into your home.

Harvesting garden flowers

The best time to cut garden flowers is early morning or evening. Cutting at these times will incur the least amount of stress on the flower, while blossoms cut in the heat of the day will wilt more quickly. A sharp knife, clean floral scissors or bypass pruners make the cleanest cuts. Take a bucket of water with you into the garden and put stems into it as soon as they are cut. When indoors recut the stems and let them soak in a cool, dark place for 4 to 6 hours.

Care for Special Flowers

Daffodils and narcissus

When freshly picked, daffodils exude a milky sap that will kill other flowers if placed a vase with them. Keep these flowers separate for at least a few hours and then change the water before using with other flowers.

Poppies, asclepias, euphorbia and others flowers with sap

Some flower stems exude a sticky sap when cut. For flowers with sap, burn stem ends in a flame for 30 seconds or dip into boiling water for 20 to 30 seconds. Be sure to cover the heads of the flowers and keep them out of the steam from the water.

Roses

Roses are a mainstay in floral design. When purchasing roses, look for fresh, pristine foliage and buds that are beginning to open. Roses are measured by stem length and petal count. A longer stem will be more expensive, but not necessarily more desirable for arranging. A blossom's petal count and head size will give you an idea of just how much space the flowers will need in the arrangement. The larger and fuller the blossom, the more lush and full; a smaller, sleek flower head requires more flowers or a more spare design.

To condition roses, remove any foliage that will be below the water line and give a sharp, slanted cut to the stem. Thorns may be removed with a sharp knife or scissors, but blossoms will last longer if the thorns are left intact.

Tulips

Tulips are becoming available almost all year long, and can add color and movement to a design. To prevent drooping stems, wrap tulips in paper (newspaper, paper bag, etc.) when they first come home, cut 1 to 2 inches from the bottom stem, and let them sit upright in cool water for a few hours. Once in an arrangement, tulips will grow toward the light, sometimes by several inches. Allow for this when placing stems and enjoy the excitement of seeing them move.

Roses with a high petal count (such as double roses) take up more space in an arrangement, so fewer stems are needed.

SECRET
Before arranging, tulips may be wrapped in paper to keep the stems straight.

VASES AND CONTAINERS

Vases and containers come in a myriad of choices, from traditional to modern. Think about the *where*, *when*, and *why* for your arrangement and select the container accordingly. Keep your eye out for suitable vases and containers as you travel through shops, yard sales, and flea markets. The most important thing is to be sure that your vase does not leak and to protect your table from any potential water leaks. First check your vases on a kitchen counter to make sure there is no leakage, and use coasters or mats between the container and any wood surface.

A good way to sort out the vase

When storing containers, group them by color to make it easy to find a particular vase. They will also look attractive if stored on an open shelf.

question is to think of size and shape. Long, low containers are good for table designs while taller vases elevate your flowers to be more visible in larger spaces or to show off a special blossom. Neutral colors work well with any flower combination and in any season.

Vases come in many colors and to ease confusion, I often choose green! Green makes a good color for flower containers because the green tones blend well with foliage and help to unify arrangements with their vases. There are many tones of green from bright yellow/green to soft blue/gray/green. Choose your vase color according to the feeling you wish to create with your flowers.

Baskets create a natural mood and compliment many varieties of flowers. Make sure that your basket has a waterproof liner and is completely water tight. Baskets may be lined with a double layer of plastic or smaller vases may be used inside the basket.

Glass vases require special care because the entire flower is visible. Stems and foliage must be carefully considered when working with glass vases. Still, they are my favorites and come in a great variety of sizes and shapes.

Look for vases on shopping trips or online. Garden centers, discount stores, flea markets, and decorator shops are all good sources for containers.

Photo by Rob Cardillo

Glass vases show both stems and flowers.

JaneGodshalk.com

Larger branches may be cut at an angle and split down the center for better water intake.

Cut stems at a sharp angle to allow for more water absorption.

Stems with nodes should be cut above the node at a sharp angle

SECRET

A 1/4- to 1/2- teaspoon of bleach added to a quart of water can keep the water looking fresh and clear, or simply change the water daily. Your flowers are, in fact, already dying the moment you cut them—fresh water will help them looking good until they're ready for the compost pile.

CUTTING BRANCHES

Many varieties of branches are available from gardens, markets, and even online. Once dried, branches may be stored and reused. In a small space, a plastic waste basket filled with a few branches may be tucked inside a closet or garage for future use. Some favorite branches of mine are birch, kiwi, manzanita, gold manzanita, and various types of dogwood (like red- and yellow-twig types).

STEM CARE AND WATER CONDITIONING

Both store-bought flowers and those from your garden will last longer when properly conditioned. When flowers come home from a supermarket, they should be given a fresh cut (at least 1/2 to 1 inch long) at a slant and put into cool water. The slanted cut allows for more water absorption. Flowers with nodes, such as carnations, should be cut *above* the node. Remove any foliage below the water line to prevent decay. This can cause dirty water and hasten the decomposition of flowers.

You should also pay attention to watering your flowers. Plain tap water is fine, but you can "condition" the water in a variety of ways. In most cases, water should be cool to extend the life of flowers. When you need flowers to open a bit sooner for a special occasion, use slightly warmer water.

Store-bought bouquets often come with little packets of flower food which can help stave off the inevitable fading of the blossoms for a few days. Keep in mind, however, that some powdered conditioners can make your water cloudy and must be used in the proportions suggested on the packet. This is fine for solid or opaque vases, but may cause a film in glass vases.

Tough, hairy stems of sunflowers will turn water cloudy quickly. To prevent this, change water daily and cut 1/2 to 1 inch from bottom of stem.

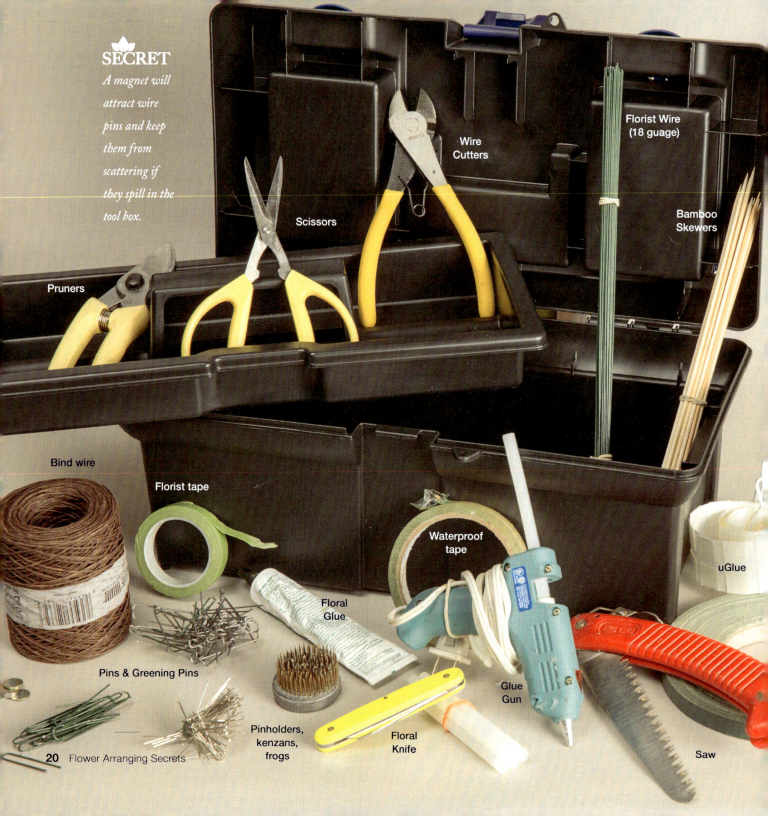

TOOLS AND MECHANICS

Choosing and organizing tools and equipment for flower arranging may be overwhelming. My favorite way to manage tools is in a traditional tool kit. Small bags and baskets are also good as are plastic containers and even shoe boxes. The important thing is to keep your tools clean and accessible.

A standard size tool kit will carry all that you need to create floral designs.

Cutting tools

- Scissors or floral snips are good for cutting flower stems.
- Pruners are necessary to cut larger branches.
- Saws are good for very large branches
- Floral knives may be used to cut flower stems and will come in handy for other things.
- Wire cutters are important to save clippers from dulling by cutting wires.

Attaching tools

- Waterproof tape (clear and green)
- Florist tape
- Bind wire
- Floral glue (cold glue)
- Glue gun (hot glue)

Supporting tools

- Bamboo skewers
- Florist wire (18 gauge)
- Pins and greening pins
- Pinholders/kenzans/frogs

Bottom layer of tool kit holds larger items

Cutting tools and skewers fit well into the top drawer

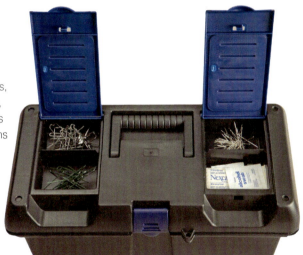

The tool kit lid holds pins, fern pins, alcohol wipes, and band-aids. Magnets hold together metal items to keep them tidy.

It is a good idea to keep alcohol wipes for cleaning tools and also band-aids in case of a cut or scratch.

Fill your tool kit with these items and you are ready to proceed with all of the designs in this book. Most all of these tools may be purchased from a local garden center, florist, or online.

SECRET

I like tools (or their handles) to be in bright colors, such as yellow or red, to make sure that they can be easily found if left in the garden or on a counter.

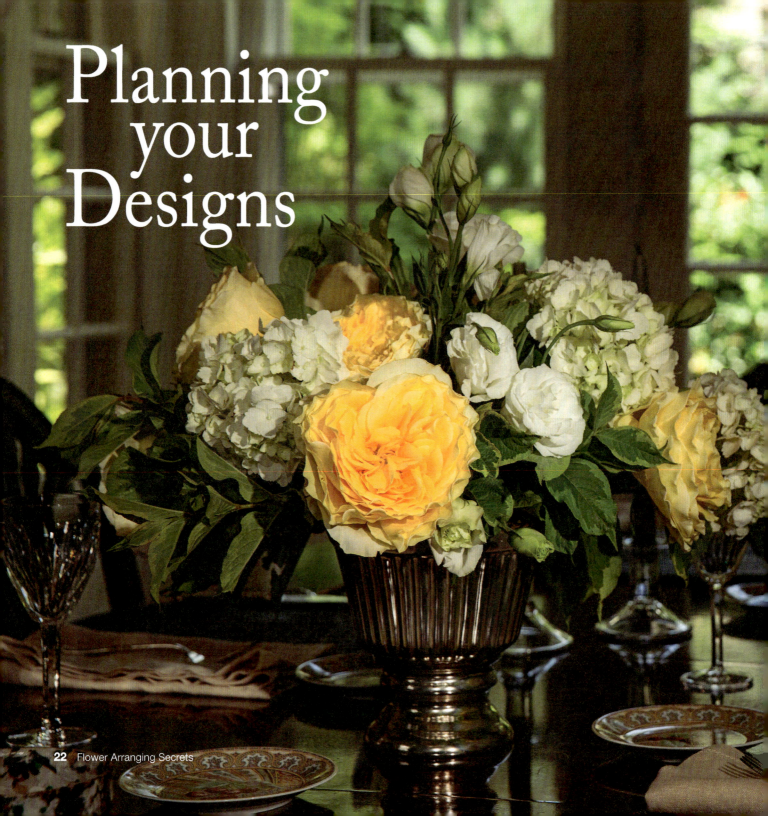

Planning your Designs

DESIGNS FOR EVENTS
A dining table set for a party

N

ow comes the fun part—finding inspiration. Inspiration may come from necessity such as an event party, or simply the desire to create an arrangement with beautiful flowers.

When an event spurs the need for a flower design, the space and spirit of the event dictate the size, colors, and style appropriate for the arrangement. An intimate dinner party needs an understated arrangement, while a larger event may need a grand display.

When it's the flower that is the driving force behind a design, the size, shape, color, and texture of the flower help decide how to use them. When the flower is the star, it is important not to add too many other elements to detract from its beauty.

JaneGodshalk.com

DESIGNS INSPIRED BY FLOWERS
A few exotic peonies were the inspiration for this design

SECRET

The well-planned size and mood of an arrangement will enhance any setting, but allow for serendipity into your ideas as well. In this picture a low container of peonies is perfect for an intimate dinner.

SPACE

You'll first need to consider the size of your space where flowers will be placed. A larger space needs a large display and a smaller area does best with a smaller arrangement. Is the arrangement for the dining room, kitchen table or counter, a hallway table or living room, or at bedside? Also consider the season—spring, summer, fall, winter, or a holiday.

STYLE

Consider the desired look or feeling:

- **Decorative**
  Round, oval, horizontal, vertical—consider the "shape" you're after.
- **Naturalistic**
  Create an "in the garden" feel using local flowers from a farmers market or those from your backyard.
- **Modern**
  Design "lean" with a few flowers to create a great impact

DESIGNS FOR JUST THE RIGHT PLACE

This rose bouquet with straw sickles fits perfectly with an icon picture above a hall table.

JaneGodshalk.com

COLOR creates the mood and complements your décor

A look at the traditional color wheel will help to organize your color choices. The three strongest colors are our primary colors: red, blue, and yellow. Between these primary colors lie secondary colors, green, orange, and violet, and between these secondary colors are tertiary colors.

What's important to know about using these colors is that colors which are further from each other on the color wheel will have more contrast, while thoses near to one another on the color wheel have less contrast.

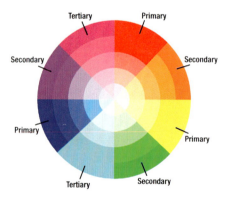

When using the color wheel you will find that it also divides into warm and cool colors. Blue and violet are most often cool, while red and orange flowers will give a warm feeling. Bright yellow adds light, while green comes in many hues from soft and cool to bright and cheerful.

COMPLEMENTARY COLORS
These are opposite on the color wheel and have strong contrast

Some classic pairs of complementary colors:
- Blue and orange
- Red and green
- Purple and yellow

Complementary colors, red and green, balance one another in a modern "lean" design (one using just a few flowers). A large amount of green balances the strong red.

ANALOGOUS COLORS
These are adjacent on the color wheel and give subtle contrast

SECRET
Newly cut autumn foliage will stay fresh in an arrangement for a few days. To extend its ornamental life, mist with water or a flower-preservative spray.

Anagolous colors of orange, yellow, and red create an autumn mood.

Analogous colors of yellow and green with accents of orange are bright and lively.

MONOCHROMATIC COLORS
These are tints and tones of one color

Using spring blossoms in various shades of pink creates a romantic feeling.

🍀 SECRET

It is easier to work flowers into an arrangement using colors closer together on the color wheel.

Monochromatic and analogous colors work more easily together than contrasting colors.

JaneGodshalk.com

STEM PLACEMENT

Radial: stems radiating out from a central point

Parallel: stems running parallel

Radial vs. Parallel stem placement

Using *radial* stem placement, all stems radiate from one binding point. This point is where the stems meet, usually just below the rim of the vase.

Radial design

Using *parallel* stem placement, each stem has its own binding point or point of emergence. The parallel designs in this book use sand or a pinholder for flower support to allow the stems to rise directly from the bottom of the vase in parallel manner.

Parallel design

JaneGodshalk.com

PROPORTIONS

The height and width of an arrangement—its proportions—will be determined by the size of the space where a design will be placed, its function and the container used.

- Table arrangements require low designs or designs with only a few narrow branches rising from a low container.
- Large spaces require arrangements with height to make a statement.

Rules for proportion, just like rules for today's fashion, are constantly evolving. A general suggestion is to think of the container as one third of the design and the flowers as making up the other two thirds. In contemporary arrangements, this is often switched with the container taking up the larger proportion and the flowers less.

My advice for home floral designs is to make the arrangement in proportions that are pleasing to your eye and fit into your specific space.

A long, low vase works well for a rectangular table and makes conversation easy at a small dinner party. This shape also may be used on a mantel.

Tall slender vases make beautiful containers for bouquets and are best displayed on hall tables, side boards, and counters.

A round bowl of flowers suits a round or square table

Tall, slender vases display flowers with drama and elegance for sideboards, counters, and buffet tables.

SECRET

The white stems shown above are "midolino", which are slender, pliable sticks tied with wire at the tips to create graceful space and enhance the proportion of the bouquet.

The Design Studio

Once you have found your inspiration, it is time to get to work—*or play!* In the following demonstrations, you will find techniques that can help cultivate your design needs and tastes.

DESIGNING WITH BRANCHES
Spring branches and flowers in pottery vase

A grid of crossed branches may be used to support flower stems.

Crossing branch stems is very simple to do and is a wonderful, natural support for flowers. Make sure to get enough branches into the vase in a criss-cross manner.

Materials
- Large pottery or ceramic vase
- Branches
- Blossoming branches
    - Viburnum
    - Peonies
    - Hydrangea

Steps

1. Make a grid from branches by crossing stems and laying one or more branches across top of vase.

2. Add viburnum with their stems crossing in a radial fashion.

3. Add hydrangea and peonies, continuing radial pattern.

4. Fresh plant material will be very thirsty, check water level frequently.

All of these flowers are supported by the crossed-branch grid.

SECRET

When choosing branches to support your arrangements, look for larger stems for larger vases and smaller, more delicate branches for smaller designs. Save the branches for fututre designs.

Three rectangular vases hold magnolia and Bradford pear branches, and support four bunches of tulips in multiple colors. Tulip stems are placed carefully to radiate from a central point.

SECRET

Place your stronger colors at the base of the design. Here, I used hot pink and orange to anchor the other colors.

JaneGodshalk.com

ROSES AND GARDEN FLOWERS WITH GRAPE VINE

This simple design creates a garden feeling, an effect accentuated by placing a glass vase into a basket. It not only gives a means to support the flowers, but also keeps the basket from leaking. The little vase of vines can be reused and washed in the dishwasher with the vines still inside.

Materials
- Basket
- Small round vase
- Grape vine
- Kiwi branch
- Roses, 3 to 5 stems
- Branches. 2 to 3 stems Stewartia or any slender branch
- Clematis, 1 stem
- Allium, 3 to 5 stems
- Astilbe, 3 to 5 stems

Steps
1. Wind grape vine into round glass vase to create support and structure.
2. Fill vase with water. Place glass vase into basket.
3. Add kiwi branches horizontally on one side.
4. Add branches of greens, one longer stem on side of kiwi branch:
    - One shorter stem on opposite side
    - Add more greens in back
5. Add roses with one behind the next, slightly off center from front of basket.
6. Fill in with allium and astilbe.
7. Add clematis.

SECRET

The round glass vase with grape vine wrapped inside, has been in my flower room for several years. It goes into the dishwasher when flowers have been removed and comes out sparking clean. Don't try to get the vines out of the bowl without cutting them or the vase may break.

JaneGodshalk.com   43

Grape-vine stems create a grid to hold flowers

SUMMER FLOWERS IN A GLASS VASE
Grape vine support

Materials
- Round glass vase
- Grape vine or willow
- Millet
- Spray roses
- Dahlias
- Queen Anne's lace

Steps

1. Fill bowl with vine in all directions.

2. Place millet with stems crossing in center of bowl.

3. Place roses in crossing pattern.

4. Place dahlias in crossing pattern, slightly asymmetrically.

5. Add filler flower.

The same procedure works with three small square vases that can be put together and used as a group or placed into a basket for another look. (See next page.)

JaneGodshalk.com

A series of square glass vases form a horizontal display for a long table

FALL FLOWERS IN SMALL SQUARE VASES

In this arrangement, leaves, chrysanthemum, bronze calla lilies, and sunflowers fill three glass vases, and can work separately or as a group. The vases are filled with grape vine from a wreath as in the design on the previous page. Bind wire is used to tie small pieces of vine to keep them from escaping from the square vase.

Ties with bind wire keep vines in the vase.

Put three small vases together in a basket for a more compact design.

JaneGodshalk.com

SECRET

Make sure that any tree bark placed in a vase has been thoroughly cleaned. Rinsing in a kitchen strainer is a good way to remove dirt and dust.

BRANCHES AND BARK

For me, searching for branches and bark is an ongoing process—and a fun one, too! Taking a walk in the woods or through my neighborhood helps me find unlimited supplies of natural materials for flower arranging. Here's one that involves using bark in a vase as a support for hydrangea, allium, and roses.

Placing pieces of tree bark into a vase will easily create flower supports and adds a natural feel to an otherwise modern setting.

JaneGodshalk.com

BRANCHES, BARK AND GERBERA

True confession: On several occasions, I have tried to grow the small tree Harry Lauder's walking stick (*Corylus avellana* 'Contorta') and so far, none have been able to survive our hot summers and cold winters in US Zone 6. The loss of the plant is less painful when the branches are used to enhance a flower arrangemnt.

MATERIALS
- Rectangular glass vase
- Bark pieces, carefully rinsed
- Branches of Harry Lauder's walking stick
- 2 to 3 stems of hydrangea
- 5 to 6 stems of gerbera
- 2 to 3 stems of alstromeria

Tree bark and Harry Lauder's walking stick in a glass vase

Add 2 to 3 stems of hydrangea

Add 5 to 6 stems of gerbera

Add 3 stems of alstromeria

Supermarket flowers and a few garden hydrangea fill a low glass vase.

SECRET

Fresh stems of hydrangea will sometimes wilt once cut from the bush. When this happens, try soaking the entire flower head in water for 6 to 8 hours to get the blossom to perk up.

DESIGNING WITH CHICKEN WIRE

The best material for supporting long stems in a loose, graceful way is chicken wire, which allows for small to large mass designs. Chicken wire (sometimes called poultry netting) may be purchased from a hardware store or online, and comes in both silver metal and coated green. Mesh holes of about 1 inch work well for most stems, but 2-inch openings will be most suitable for heavy stemmed flowers.

When working with chicken wire, attach it with tape to the top of a container making a grid for flower stems, or fold into a vase giving multiple spaces for stem support. For larger vases, extend the wire above the rim of the container about an inch or two. Smaller, low designs may have the wire inside the vase.

Branches and flowers that have harder stems are best for chicken wire structures and care must be taken with softer stems, such as daffodils and tulips, when inserting them through the wire holes. You don't want to accidentally bend or break the stems.

Cut the chicken wire with wire cutters (large tin snips make work the easiest, but regular wire cutters will do), and measure a size of wire to be cut two to three times the size of the container opening. Fill the vase with water after the wire has been inserted. First add branches and larger flowers, then smaller flowers. When the arrangement is wilted and ready for the compost pile, the stems may be removed and the wire washed in the dishwasher for reuse.

A green and white color theme works during any season of the year.

JaneGodshalk.com

A casual lunch *al fresco* can be enhanced by a low container filled with spring flowers.

A closed tulip blossom can be "reflexed" into an open position. You do this by bending individual petals backwards with your thumb.

SPRING FLOWERS IN CHICKEN WIRE

Materials
- Long, low container
- Chicken wire
- 3 to 5 stems of lilacs
- 2 to 3 stems of viburnum
- 2 to 3 stems of hellebores
- 5 to 7 tulips

Steps
1. Cut chicken wire to 2 to 3 times size of container and fold pieces of cut wire into container.
2. Add lilac stems at angles with all stems radiating from one point in vase.
3. Add viburnum in same fashion.
4. Place hellebores and tulips with all stems radiating from a central point in the design.
5. Tulip blossoms may be "reflexed". A closed tulip blossom can be reflexed into an open position. You do this by bending individual petals backwards with your thumb.

SECRET

All radial designs work best when each stem is placed as if it is coming from a central point. Think of them as light beams radiating out from the sun.

JaneGodshalk.com

LARGE DESIGN IN CHICKEN WIRE

Large-scale designs may be done with the same chicken wire techniques. This design looks impressive, but is quite simple. The opulent peonies and spring branches fill a clay urn quickly and easily.

SECRET

"It's hard to go wrong when working with spring flowers, but they are less hardy and have a shorter life span than flowers grown later in the season. Don't create a spring arrangement more than one day ahead of your party or event."

Spring in the eastern US is a season when we get to enjoy beautiful blossoming trees, shrubs and peonies. Here azalea, variegated weigela, and peonies (all from my own garden, with a few peonies borrowed from a neighbor) fill a rustic urn. Chicken wire keeps the branches and flowers in place.

JaneGodshalk.com

Once you try this leaf folding technique, you will want to use it over and over again. It turns a flat leaf into a rounded form.

FOLDING LEAVES IN A CHICKEN WIRE ARRANGEMENT

Aspidistra leaves are a favorite of mine, as they can be folded, pleated, stripped or just left in their beautiful natural form. The slight pleat where the leaf meets the stem creates an elegant look. I keep an aspidistra houseplant at home, just in case I run out of those I can buy from the flower market.

A pedestal plate or cake plate may be used with a low bowl of flowers for an elegant, elevated effect. Folded aspidistra leaves create a ribbon-like look and fill space with shiny texture. This adds contrast to flowers.

Materials
- Pedestal plate
- Low bowl or cake-baking pan
- Chicken wire
- Tape
- Pins or staples
- 3 to 5 hydrangea
- 10 stems of spray roses
- 10 stems of lisianthus
- 10 stems of aspidistra
- 5 stems of variegated aspidistra

Choose a pedestal or cake plate—it may be glass or metal—and a low bowl, cake pan or pie plate that's slightly smaller in diameter than the pedestal plate. Fill the low bowl with a double layer of chicken wire. Tape the wire to the bowl to keep it firm.

Cut a piece of chicken wire about three times the size of the bowl.

Fold wire into bowl and attach to the sides with clear waterproof tape.

Fold leaves and staple or pin into rounded shape.

Add leaves to bowl with wire. Make sure that leaf stems all radiate from a central point in the middle of the bowl.

Vines or branches circling over an arrangement are called "overlay" and add movement and lightness to a design.

Grape vine wreath is placed on top of a bowl filled with chicken wire.

Greens are placed in groups of three, all radiating from a central point.

More greens are added to fill out circular form.

Start with one variety of flowers, all radiating from a central axis.

ROUND ARRANGEMENT IN VINE WREATH AND CHICKEN WIRE

This design is a basic one and the process of organizing stems applies to all round arrangements. Keep in mind that each inserted flower is radiating from a central binding point.

Here's a tip: Using a grape vine wreath, or a pliable branch such as willow, will make good supports for larger arrangements. Placing chicken wire inside the vase adds extra support.

Materials

- Round bowl
- Grape vine wreath
- Chicken wire
- Bind wire
- Cedar
- Hellebore foliage
- Stock
- Hydrangea
- Roses

Steps

1. Fold chicken wire into bowl. Lay vine wreath or branches over bowl. Attach wreath to wire with bind wire. Fill vase with water.
2. Add three groups of greens, with stems meeting in the center of the bowl.
3. Add flowers and other greens.
4. When insertions are completed, add a few stems of vine circling over the arrangement.

JaneGodshalk.com

DESIGNING IN SAND

Working with sand as a support for flowers is useful for straight stems in a parallel placement (you can also use a few larger stems or rooted plants). Sand is a good medium, as it holds water well and the flowers in it will last a long time. It may be purchased in hardware and building-supply stores. "Play sand" (for children's sandboxes) is better than builders' sand, as it contains fewer stones and impurities.

To get started, fill your container with sand and add water until the the sand is damp but not wet, usually about 1/3 water to 2/3 sand. If water starts to pool above the sand, add a bit more sand.

Designs in sand may be refreshed with new flowers replacing those past their prime. Disposal of sand is easy if you have a yard or garden. Just walk it out to the back of the garden and empty the vase. It will work its way into the soil quickly. Sand shouldn't be washed down a sink drain, as it might clog the pipe. You should wash the container once most of the sand has been removed.

SECRET

Making stem insertions in sand may be tricky at first. It helps to make a hole with a pick or scissors, insert the flower stem, and then fill in the hole. Make sure that your stems are deep enough in the sand to support their height.

An orchid design in sand, this one featuring bark, a few winter greens, and a shell to remind us of endless days at the beach.

JaneGodshalk.com

SECRET

Parallel arrangements can work well in a series of multiple containers running down the length of a long table. The space between parallel stems is dramatic, costs nothing, and is eco-friendly as well.

OAK BRANCH AND ALSTROMERIA IN SAND

Flower arrangements with stems placed in a parallel fashion may give a modern feel or create a more naturalistic mood. If you have a long table to fill, try two or three vases filled with sand and flowers. Keep the arrangement uncluttered if you want your guests to see through the designs.

Materials
- Low containers
- Play sand and water
- 3 or 4 branches
- 3 or 4 stems of alstromeria
- 8 to 3 stems of zebra or other grass

1. Fill low container with play sand, add water until damp (about 1/3 water to 2/3 sand).

2. Add branches in two groups at each end of the containers, one group slightly taller than the other.

3. Add alstromeria or other straight-stemmed flower.

4. Add grasses or other wispy material.

A natural, outdoors feeling is created when stems are inserted in a "parallel" fashion, each stem placed as if it were growing in a garden.

Spring Flowers in Sand

Spring flowers are wonderful for parallel designs, as it gives us a feeling of being in a delightful spring garden.

SECRET
Fragrance is an important part of designing with spring flowers. Hyacinth, lilies, and narcissus have strong aromas and are better used in large open spaces, not intimate dinner tables. Be careful when using allium, which may have a pungent fragrance.

Materials
- Long, low vase
- Play sand
- Bamboo skewers
- Florist tape
- Branches
    - 8 to 12 stems of pussy willow
- 4 to 6 stems of daffodils or narcissus
- 1 to 2 of hyacinth
- 6 to 8 stems of muscari
- Poppies or tulips

Steps
1. Fill vase with sand and add water until damp, not wet.
2. Insert branches in groups with space in between.
3. Stake daffodils with bamboo skewer inside of stem.
4. Stake stems of hyacinth and wrap muscari into groups of 3 to 5 stems each.
5. Insert hyacinth and muscari.
6. Insert poppies or tulips.
7. Water the arrangement when the sand seems to dry out. Fading flowers may be replaced with fresh stems.

Narcissus or daffodils will need to be staked in order to hold the stems upright when placed into the sand.

Small flowers, such as muscari, work best when several stems are taped together on a bamboo skewer.

ORCHIDS IN SAND

This is a favorite winter design for me, as it will last for weeks and looks very dramatic. Make sure to spray the orchid roots frequently, at least every other day, and keep the sand moist.

Materials
- Long low vase
- Bark or branch
- 1 or 2 orchid plants (such as the readily available *Phalaenopsis* moth orchid)

Steps
1. Fill container with sand and water.
2. Lay branch or bark over sand.
3. Lay orchid plants onto sand and bark and support the stem with the branch if it needs it.
4. If your orchid blossom has a stem that is too long for your vase, the bloom may be cut and placed in the sand. It will not last nearly as long.

JaneGodshalk.com

Multiple Containers
Here are a series of glass vases filled with purple and pink flowers of anemone, chives, hellebores, and sweet William. They are combined with a bunch of asparagus and artichoke candles to fill a kitchen table.

DESIGNING "LEAN"

Use fewer flowers and more space between vases to create impact. This allows each stem or variety of flower to speak for itself and be part of a grouping to create a competed design. An economical way to use flowers is to take advantage of space—this gives the eye a resting place and costs nothing to fill.

JaneGodshalk.com

Three glass vases hold one bunch of kale (about 5 stems), a bunch of dahlias (about 8 stems), and a few stems of grasses

SECRET

Arranging in multiple vases allow for flowers to be moved easily from place to place, such as from a kitchen counter to a dining room table.

DESIGNS IN GLASS

Just a few flowers
Two stems of long-lasting anthurium with contrasting red and green colors combine with folded aspidistra leaves in a glass vase.

SECRET
Sunflowers are heliotropic, meaning that when they're in the garden, their faces follow the sun. Once cut, the flower head will remain in the same position.

Sunflowers

One bunch of sunflowers from the supermarket and a few stems of grass from the garden make a strong display. The trick to arranging sunflowers is *not* to arrange them. Just let them gracefully fall where they would like to be. Sunflowers have hairy stems and the water will need changing almost daily.

DESIGNS WITH A KENZAN OR PIN HOLDER

Three stems of peony from a local grower are all that is needed for a stunning table display. Two pinholders are placed into a low vase and stems held by the pins. (A guest at the table thought that they were held up by "magic!")

SECRET

Pinholders are used in Japansese Ikebana flower arranging and called Kenzans. They may be purchased online and used over and over again. There is no better or easier way to show off a few special flowers.

HAND-TIED BOUQUET

The best example of a radial floral design is the hand-tied bouquet. Although creating one with ease takes practice, it is a good way to get stems to support flowers in a vase. A tidy spiral makes both stems and flowers look their best in a glass vase.

The hand-tied bouquet begins with the careful cleaning and ordering of all flower and foliage stems. (**IMPORTANT:** Any leaves that that will be below the binding point must be removed.) Organize materials into groups.

AN AUTUMN HAND-TIED BOUQUET

Simple hand-tied bouquet (using four varieties of flowers and three varieties of foliage)

Materials

Large round flowers:
- 4 hydrangea
- Small round flowers:
    - 10 to 12 stems of roses
    - 6 to 10 stems of dahlia, zinnia, or chrysanthemum

Filler flowers:
- 6 to 10 stems of crocosmia, berry, or other small flower

Foliage:
- 3 to 5 stems of sweet gum leaves or other foliage

1. Clean flower and foliage stems and lay out in groups.

2. Start with one stem in your left hand if you are right handed (and right hand if you are a lefty). Pick up a second stem with the opposite hand and lay on top of the first in a cross pattern.

3. Continue to add flowers by crossing the stems to the left and turning the bouquet a quarter turn to the right with each additional stem.

4. When the bouquet is completed, its stems will form a radial pattern.

5. Tie stems with bind wire and cut them to the same length.

Put completed design into vase

SECRET

Making a hand-tied bouquet is not much of a secret. It simply takes time and practice to create a proper spiral. If the process is not working out for you, simply take the stems and insert them into your vase in a radial fashion.

JaneGodshalk.com

Chartreuse green is a wonderful color for showing off bright flowers.

SUMMER HAND-TIED BOUQUETS

Materials
- Hydrangea
- Green chrysanthemum
- Green thistle
- Orange roses
- Orange celosia
- Purple kale
- Hyacinth beans

"Hand-tied bouquets make great gifts because they are easy to transport and may be used in any space."

All stems cross in radial fashion.

The spiral expands as more stems are added to the spiral.

A few vertical stems of veronica give this bouquet an airy touch. If you don't have veronica available, substitute astilbe, grasses, or other light and airy material.

Above: Another simple bouquet done in the same fashion holds the following materials:
- Geranium foliage
- Spray roses
- Astrantia
- Veronica

Folds of white handmade paper, along with gold Manzanita branches and pine cones, last a long time in winter when flowers are typically expensive.

HAND-TIED BOUQUET FOR WINTER

Using this fun technique, you employ paper folds to add movement. Gold Manzanita branches entwine with white narcissus and folds of white handmade paper to create a modern holiday bouquet. Gold pine cones enhance the design.

SECRET
Paper forms can be made in any color, and added when a non-floral element is desired. Paper in earth tone colors work very well, too.

Spread hot glue, or glue dots, down the center of folded paper and place a wire over the glue. Fold paper over wire and fold into graceful flower forms.

JaneGodshalk.com

FRUITS AND VEGETABLES

Just a few tricks will make long lasting fruits and vegetables fun and attractive additions to your arrangements.

JaneGodshalk.com

Green grapes and green apples make a good foundation for dark purple viburnum berries and white lisianthus

GRAPES AND FLOWERS

A terracotta pot is filled with grapes, apples and flowers in soft, monochromatic colors. Dark viburnum berries give this late-summer arrangement contrast of light and dark.

The weight of two bunches of grapes balance each other when wired to a bamboo skewer.

Close up of wired grapes.

Two bamboo skewers placed at an angle make apples easy to insert into a design.

Materials
- 2 bunches of grapes
- 3 apples
- 3 stems of lemon leaf (salal)
- 3 viburnum branches
- 7 stems of lisianthus
- 3 stems of celosia

Steps
1. This container is a terracotta planter with a hole for drainage at the bottom. It has been lined with a plastic bowl to be water tight.
2. Fill bowl with chicken wire.
3. Add grapes by wiring each bunch across the bowl with bamboo picks and tape.
4. Add salal leaves and viburnum branches in radial fashion.
5. Add apples.
6. Add celosia.
7. Add lisianthus.

JaneGodshalk.com

Pomegranates and Pine cones

Materials
- 3 branches of holly
- 3 branches of pine or other evergreen
- 3 pomegranates
- 5 to 6 red roses
- pine cones
- 5 stems of astrantia or baby's breath

Steps
1. Fill container with chicken wire and water.
2. Add evergreens and holly.
3. Add roses.
4. Put picks into pomegranates; wire pine cones; add to flowers and greens.

Long, low arrangements are perfect for rectangular tables and mantels.

Add greens first, contrasting rough and shiny textures.

Pine cones may be wired individually or in groups

SECRET
In a long, low arrangement such as this, stems are still inserted in a radial manner. Each stem is slightly turned from a central binding point.

SECRET

To preserve fruits and vegetables longer in arrangements, soak them in a solution of floor polish, which is actually acrylic. Use 1/3 polish to 2/3 water. Make sure that none of the preserved foods are eaten.

Large, heavy fruits and vegetables are placed at the base of the design. Fresh flowers may be changed several times while fruits and vegetables will last longer.

Harvest Vegetables

A low bowl filled with seasonal fruits and vegetables makes a long lasting arrangement for an autumn table or kitchen counter.

Materials
- 1 small watermelon or squash
- 1 large red onion
- 1 purple cabbage cut into star shape
- 1 bunch of purple grapes
- 1 bunch of red grapes
- 1 stem of milkweed, asclepias
- 1 stem of kale
- 2 to 3 stems of celosia
- 1 stem of salal or other foliage
- 2 stems of chrysanthemums

Steps

Overnight: Cut cabbage across the top into six segments. Make sure only to cut the cabbage about 2/3 of the way down or it will fall apart.

1. Fill bowl with chicken wire and an inch or two of water.
2. Add largest fruits and vegetables first—watermelon, onion, cabbage.
3. Add smaller materials—kale, grapes, leaves, and milkweed.
4. Add flowers—celosia and chrysanthemum.

JaneGodshalk.com

More Secrets

We've covered a lot of ground so far, but here are a few extra design and botanical tips that you will find helpful.

SECRET

Echeveria is a succulent plant that is long lasting and may be purchased at garden centers. They may be rooted plants or cut. Once cut from their roots store them in a vase or bowl with sand and water very occasionally. They will be available to use in your arrangements whenever you need them.

TABLE DISPLAY

A series of low containers makes a dramatic display for tables. Low metal containers are filled with flowers and plants while small ceramic vases hold just a few flowers.

Metal container holds four small begonia plants, and glass vases with a few roses and chrysanthemum. Wisps of cedar fill in the empty spaces.

SECRET

Small glass vases placed between potted plants in a low container can be cleaned and refilled with fresh flower stems. This can keep an arrangement looking perfect indefinitely.

Similar components may be used in a round table setting.

JaneGodshalk.com

COLOR

Bright colors of zinnias growing in a field are softened by lots of green foliage.

SECRET

Zinnia stems are hollow and very fragile. Cut them at a sharp angle with very sharp scissors or knife and insert into arrangements by holding the stem at the base.

How do I know what color is the right one?

Look to nature. Color is the first thing that captures the eye in a floral design. Each color brings thoughts of seasonal inspiration, personal preference, and emotion. Colors go in and out of popularity, and may follow the international fashion trends (Google the word "Pantone" to see the latest colors used by top fashion designers).

In many flowers, there are multiple colors within one blossom. An orange rose may have purple undertones on the outer blossoms, while a lily may have darker tones in its throat and pollen that changes from yellow to rust. And multi-toned flowers, such as alstromeria, have multiple colors in each flower head. Look to these undertone colors for good choices for other flowers in an arrangement.

Left: A row of vibrant zinnias growing in a garden gives inspiration to an arrangement with similar color balance.

Multiple colors of zinnias are softened by pale, mint-green foliage.

JaneGodshalk.com

FOLIAGE

How do I effectively use leaves and foliage in my designs?

There are a myriad of choices for flowers and foliage for floral designs. Selecting the right material for each design makes executing the larger arrangement much easier.

A. Fresh wheat and many other grasses have straight stems and are good for vertical lines. Other types of foliage with straight lines include iris leaves and flax.

B. Its cascading heads and the downward leaf angles make millet a good choice for covering the edges of vases.

C. The glossy green of hellebore foliage provides contrast and a resting place for the eye. Aspidistra, dracaena, philodendron, rhododendron, holly, and galex are some other greens with shiny textures.

D. With lots of little needles, cedar has a feathery quality and is good for filling spaces in a design. It may be staked with a branch to be used vertically, or left in its natural cascading habit.

A.

B.

D.

SECRET

Evergreens are wonderful, long lasting filler plants. Look for pine, boxwood, and spruce to enhance your designs.

Flower Identification

1. Allium
2. Astrantia
3. Anthurium
4. Calla
5. Celosia
6. Chives
7. Chrysanthemum
8. Daffodil
9. Dalhia
10. Delphiniium
11. Gerbera
12. Hellebore
13. Hyacinth
14. Hydrangea

15. Kale
16. Lisianthus
17. Orchid
18. Peony
19. Queen Anne's Lace
20. Rose
21. Sunfllower
22. Sweet William
23. Thistle
24. Tulip
25. Veronica
26. Viburnum
27. Viburnum berry
28. Zinnia

JaneGodshalk.com

About the Author

Jane Godshalk teaches floral design on the faculty of Longwood Gardens, one of the nation's finest botanical gardens. She lectures across the country and in Europe. She has studied extensively in Europe and the United States, and is a member of the American Institute of Floral Designers (AIFD).

Among her numerous awards are the Garden Club of America's prestigious national medal for "consistently innovative floral design," and the American Horticultural Society's Great American Gardener Award for "significant contributions to floral design education in publications, on the platform, and to the public."

Her website is *janegodshalk.com*

CPSIA information can be obtained
at www.ICGtesting.com
Printed in the USA
BVXC01n1617230314
348458BV00001B/1